Legendary Scientists: The Life and Legacy of Galileo Galilei

By Charles River Editors

About Charles River Editors

Charles River Editors was founded by Harvard and MIT alumni to provide superior editing and original writing services, with the expertise to create digital content for publishers across a vast range of subject matter. In addition to providing original digital content for third party publishers, Charles River Editors republishes civilization's greatest literary works, bringing them to a new generation via ebooks.

Introduction

Galileo (1564-1642)

"What has philosophy got to do with measuring anything? It's the mathematicians you have to trust..." – Galileo

It would be impossible to overstate the accomplishments and legacy of a man history has dubbed the "Father of Modern Science". In his lifetime, Galileo straddled the epochs of the Renaissance and the Scientific Revolution, and it was his work and technological advances that helped usher in a brand new understanding of the solar system and the scientific method. Stephen Hawking himself has asserted, "Galileo, perhaps more than any other single person, was responsible for the birth of modern science."

Of course, part of what made Galileo such a monumental figure was the fact that he was ahead of his time, and that he mostly refused to conform to the accepted dogmas of contemporary society. As he once put it, "Philosophy is written in that great book which ever lies before our eyes — I mean the universe — but we cannot understand it if we do not first learn the language and grasp the symbols, in which it is written. This book is written in the mathematical language, and the symbols are triangles, circles and other geometrical figures, without whose help it is impossible to comprehend a single word of it."

Galileo has been one of history's most famous and influential scientists ever since his life and death over 350 years ago, but it's somewhat ironic that he might be best known for being subjected to the Inquisition and for making a comment that he almost certainly never said. His insistence in defending Copernicus' heliocentric solar system led to charges of heresy, even though he attempted to square his heliocentric system with Scripture and offered up St. Augustine's teachings as a partial defense. In private, however, Galileo was far more scathing, at one point writing in a private letter to fellow astronomer Johannes Kepler in 1610, "My dear Kepler, what would you say of the learned here, who…have steadfastly refused to cast a glance through the telescope? What shall we make of this? Shall we laugh, or shall we cry?" And according to a legend that refuses to die, Galileo refused to recant; after being charged with heresy, sentenced to imprisonment, and having his books banned, Galileo allegedly uttered, "And yet it moves", in a barely veiled reference to the Earth moving around the Sun.

Galileo may not have challenged authority as the legend holds, but he was undeterred by house arrest. He continued to write almost all the way up until his death, and by the time his 77 years on Earth were finished, he had greatly improved the use of telescopes, revolutionized our understanding of the universe, made discoveries on Jupiter and Venus, posited the idea that physics was a study of mathematics, and much more.

Legendary Scientists: The Life and Legacy of Galileo Galilei profiles the life, legends, and legacy of the famous scientist, while examining his career and contributions to science and technology. Along with pictures of important people, places, and events, you will learn about Galileo like you never have before, in no time at all.

Chapter 1: Early Life and Education

"You cannot teach a man anything, you can only help him to find it within himself." - Galileo

Galileo was born in Pisa, Italy on February 15, 1564, the first of six children born to Vincenzo and Giulia Galilei. Galileo's family descended from a long class of nobles who lived in Florence with the name Bonaiuti around the 14th century, but it remains unclear how they became the middle class family with the name Galilei in the 15th or 16th century.

Little is known of Galileo's mother Giulia, but Vincenzo was a popular musician and musical theorist who specialized in playing the lute. He was also a philosophical man who took great interest in his oldest son, and it's safe to assume that Galileo inherited his interest in mathematics from his father, given the connections between musical theory and mathematics. Vincenzo named his son after a distant relative, Galileo Bonaiuti, who himself followed much of the kind of life Vincenzo planned for his son; Bonaiuti was both a doctor and well-respected professor who occasionally dabbled in politics.

As a child, Galileo learned to play the lute, a stringed instrument that was popular in the Italian court at that time. His younger brother Michelangelo became a lutenist like Vincenzo, and even though he was a renowned music composer, the musical career wouldn't pay the bills. Of course, being a doctor and professor would make Galileo's family well off, but he had other things in mind for himself.

A lute

Galileo was fortunate to have been born at the height of the Italian Renaissance, a wonderful time to be alive for a young man with a scientific bent. Vast advances were being made in the world of science, as one theory after another was being called into question, studied, confirmed or refuted. Nearly two decades before Galileo was born, Nicolaus Copernicus posthumously published writings that called into question the geocentric model of astronomy put forth over a millennium earlier by the ancient astronomer Ptolemy and the legendary philosopher Aristotle. Galileo would also count Johannes Kepler among his acquaintances during his own life.

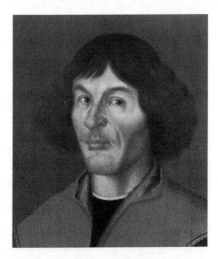

Portrait of Copernicus

Along with grand new ideas, the Italian Renaissance was a wonderful time for technological innovation as well. Da Vinci was sketching out his flying machine, while Leonard Digges was finding ways to arranged polished lenses to create a telescope. Vincenzo Galilei himself was involved in the expanding world of knowledge and creativity. When Galileo was 8, Vincenzo moved his family from Pisa to Florence, the epicenter of the Italian Revolution, and in 1581 Vincenzo published his own findings about changes and improvements in the realm of musical theory. He is remembered today for performing some of the earliest experiments in history with non-linear relation. He discovered, for instance, that the pitch of a stretched string changes in relation to the square root of the tension the string is under. Vincenzo's work was a clear demonstration to his young son that mathematics was not simply an abstract study but also related intimately to everyday life.

As a teenager, Galileo had completed his studies with the monks at the Camaldolese Monastery at Vallombrosa, Italy, and he entered the University of Pisa to study medicine. A devout

Catholic, Galileo initially entertained ideas about entering the priesthood, but he quickly realized he was more interested in science than theology. This also meant he was happy to follow his father's plans for him to go into medicine, at least at first. Galileo also had the benefit of studying under one of Italy's best physicists and botanists, Andrew Cæsalpinus.

While he enjoyed his studies in Pisa, Galileo often found his active mind wandering from the topic at hand. According to legend, Galileo took interest in the large chandelier that hung in the Pisa Cathedral. The breezes blowing in from the open windows caused it to swing back and forth, making arcs of various sizes. As Galileo watched this chandelier, he became aware that it seemed to move at the same rhythm, no matter the size of the arcs. That summer, when he should have been reading medical texts, he instead spent his time building two pendulums of different sizes to test his theory. He discovered that that the size of the pendulum would not affect the fact that it took the same amount of time to swing from one side to the other, and that a properly built pendulum would move at a constant speed. While Galileo never did much with this discovery, he did record his findings in his journal and shared his thoughts at the beginning of the 17th century. About 70 years later, Christiaan Huygens would use Galileo's findings to create one of the first consistently accurate clocks in the world.

The "lamp of Galileo" in Pisa Cathedral

Not surprisingly, it didn't take long for Galileo to realize that he was much more interested in science and mathematics than medicine, and his family had all the proof it needed of that fact. There was no question that Galileo was intelligent and a diligent worker, but he was failing most of his classes, with the exception of those dealing with mathematics. When Galileo broke the news to his father that he did not want to study medicine, Vincenzo agreed to allow him to remain at the university and study to be a mathematics professor. This may have been a bitter pill for Vincenzo to swallow, as he had always hoped his son would enter the more lucrative field of medicine, but his son also had a clear gift for math and science. Vincenzo had reluctantly let Galileo study geometry and Euclid's works while he was at school, so he was fully aware of his son's ever growing interest in math.

Unfortunately, Galileo would not remain at the University of Pisa much longer. In 1583, his father suffered a reversal in his fortunes that required his son to drop out of college and return home to Florence. But Galileo continued his experiments at home, all the while working as a tutor to help make ends meet for his family. He also set out to try to earn himself a faculty position in mathematics.

Within just three years, Galileo had perfected his first invention, a thermoscope. Using hydrostatic balance, he was able to create this ancestor of the modern thermometer. He published his findings and the details of his technique in 1586, garnering the attention of Italian scientists for the first time.

A thermoscope

Like Leonardo, Galileo also recognized a strong connection between science and art. In 1588, he completed his studies in art and began teaching at the Accademia delle Arti del Disegno in Florence. Although Galileo was not particularly artistic himself, he was still a master of perspective and contrasts of light and dark. Surrounded by the fabulous art being produced in

Florence at that time, he became fascinated with the works of Cigoli. The two became fast friends, and Cigoli later featured some of Galileo's scientific findings in his own paintings.

A painting of Cigoli

Galileo was also making waves in the literary community. During this time he attended a series of discussions at the Academy of Florence in which people tried to deduce the actual location of Dante's Inferno. Rather than approach the question philosophically, Galileo came at it from a mathematical basis. He focused his attention on the passage that said that Satan's face was about as long as and just as wide as St. Peter's "Cone" in Rome. After ascertaining its size, Galileo used the knowledge of anatomy he had gained while a medical student to calculate that the devil must have arms that were about 2,000 feet long.

Chapter 2: Professor and Inventor

Eventually, Galileo's work caused quite a stir in the academic community, and Galileo received his desired appointment as Chair of Mathematics at the University of Pisa in 1581. If anyone was bothered by the fact that he never graduated from there when he was a student, they kept their concerns to themselves.

Galileo returned to the University at an interesting time. The professors of science and mathematics, as well as their students, were involved in a hot debate over Aristotle's law of nature, which stated that heavier objects would fall faster than lighter ones. This seemed to fly in the face of the visual evidence, so Galileo ultimately decided to perform his own experiments. According to legend, one day Galileo climbed the famous 185 foot Leaning Tower of Pisa carrying a wide variety of balls. With an intrigued crowd of students and professors watching, he dropped the entire lot off the tower at the same time. Much to everyone's amazement, they all landed at the same time, disproving Aristotle's theory. Based on this and other experiments, Galileo began his first scientific paper, *De Motu* (*On Motion*), but he would never complete it.

The Leaning Tower today

Following his success with experiments in motion, Galileo became something of a celebrity around Pisa, but as is often the case with young men of great intellect, he became proud and a bit obnoxious. His explicit refutation of the revered Aristotle didn't sit well with everyone, given that Aristotle's philosophy and work had long gone unquestioned, and this was not the best move for a new professor who did not yet have tenure. He was not asked to return to Pisa when his initial term as a professor ran out in 1592.

That timing was particularly bad for Galileo, because his father had died in 1591, leaving him the head of a family that included his mother and four younger siblings. In 1592, Galileo took a post as a professor with the University of Padua, and he would spend the next 18 years there teaching geometry, astronomy and mechanics. Though most of his time was spent exploring the fundamental and applied sciences, he also spent some of his time dabbling in astrology. This was not that unusual at the time, because it was considered a valid science on par with mathematics or astronomy. He was a good teacher and regularly attracted a large number of pupils, many of whom would later take what they learned from him to new heights, both figuratively and literally. As Galileo's reputation grew, foreigners also came to see him, including Archduke Ferdinand (who later became Emperor of Germany), princes from Alsace, and Gustavus Adolphus of Sweden.

It was also around 1592 that Galileo is believed to have first come in contact with people who questioned the almost universally accepted theory that the Earth was at the center of the universe. Galileo explained the first time he heard about Copernicus' theory of a heliocentric solar system:

> "I cannot omit this opportunity of relating to you what happened to myself at the time when this opinion (the Copernican system) began to be discussed. I was then a very young man, and had scarcely finished my course of philosophy, which other occupations obliged me to leave off, when there arrived in this country, from Rostoch, a foreigner, whose name, I believe, was Christian Vurstisius (Wurteisen), a follower of Copernicus. This person delivered, on this subject, two or three lectures in a certain academy, and to a crowded audience. Believing that several were attracted more by the novelty of the subject than by any other cause, and being firmly persuaded that this opinion was a piece of solemn folly, I was unwilling to be present. Upon interrogating, however, some of those who were there, I found that they all made it a subject of merriment, with the exception of one, who assured me that it was not a thing wholly ridiculous. As I considered this individual to be both prudent and circumspect, I repented that I had not attended the lectures; and, whenever I met any of the followers of Copernicus, I began to inquire if they had always been of the same opinion. I found that there was not one of them who did not declare that he had long maintained the very opposite opinions, and had not gone over to the new doctrines till he was driven by the force of argument. I next examined them one by one, to see if they were masters of the arguments on the

opposite side; and such was the readiness of their answers, that I was satisfied they had not taken up this opinion from ignorance or vanity. On the other hand, whenever I interrogated the Peripatetics and the Ptolemeans—and, out of curiosity, I have interrogated not a few—respecting their perusal of Copernicus's work, I perceived that there were few who had seen the book, and not one who understood it. Nor have I omitted to inquire among the followers of the Peripatetic doctrines, if any of them had ever stood on the opposite side; and the result was, that there was not one. Considering, then, that nobody followed the Copernican doctrine, who had not previously held the contrary opinion, and who was not well acquainted with the arguments of Aristotle and Ptolemy; while, on the other hand, nobody followed Ptolemy and Aristotle, who had before adhered to Copernicus, and had gone over from him into the camp of Aristotle;—weighing, I say, these things, I began to believe that, if any one who rejects an opinion which he has imbibed with his milk, and which has been embraced by an infinite number, shall take up an opinion held only by a few, condemned by all the schools, and really regarded as a great paradox, it cannot be doubted that he must have been induced, not to say driven, to embrace it by the most cogent arguments. On this account I have become very curious to penetrate to the very bottom of the subject."

Of course, Galileo was not the only astronomer in Europe, and he soon came into contact with Johannes Kepler, in part due to a disagreement over the origins of Earth's tides. Although the two became friendly acquaintances, they were at odds over the source of the tides. Galileo attributed them to Earth's motion and the shape and size of Earth's bodies of water, but Kepler came up with the revolutionary (and accurate) concept that the Moon was responsible. Kepler, who would go on to revolutionize astronomy with his laws on planetary motion, was ridiculed by Galileo for his beliefs. Galileo was still talking about Kepler's theory in 1624 (about 30 years after Kepler first advanced it), writing in a 1624 letter to another friend, "Among all the great men who have philosophized about this remarkable effect, I am more astonished at Kepler than at any other. Despite his open and acute mind, and though he has at his fingertips the motions attributed to the earth, he nevertheless lent his ear and his assent to the moon's dominion over the waters, to occult properties, and to such puerilities." Albert Einstein would later note this disagreement and state, "It has always hurt me to think that Galilei did not acknowledge the work of Kepler…That, alas, is vanity…You find it in so many scientists."

A portrait of Kepler

Nevertheless, Galileo maintained a friendly relationship in Kepler, who he undoubtedly viewed as a kindred spirit. In a letter in 1596, Galileo wrote to Kepler, "I esteem myself happy to have as great an ally as you in my search for truth. I will read your work ... all the more willingly because I have for many years been a partisan of the Copernican view because it reveals to me the causes of many natural phenomena that are entirely incomprehensible in the light of the generally accepted hypothesis. To refute the latter I have collected many proofs, but I do not publish them, because I am deterred by the fate of our teacher Copernicus who, although he had won immortal fame with a few, was ridiculed and condemned by countless people (for very great is the number of the stupid)." Galileo continued teaching Ptolemy's system in Padua because he was afraid of the consequences of publicizing his support of Copernicus, an ironic concern given what would happen to him at the end of his life. But at the time, Galileo was also under pressure to provide for his family of siblings, particularly the dowries for his two sisters, which were supposed to be paid in installments during the first years of their marriages. His father had brokered this deal before he died, and it was now left to Galileo to see that it was fulfilled.

Galileo was not making enough money as a professor, which added further incentive to keep on inventing. The thermoscope that he had earlier created was not particularly profitable, nor were any of his other earlier inventions. However, in 1596 Galileo designed a type of compass that could be used by the military to both aim their cannons and determine how much gunpowder to use. This was purchased by enough Italian soldiers to provide some relief to his financial worries, and the following year he was able to modify the compass so that it could be used by civilian surveyors. By working with instrument maker Marc'Antonio Mazzoleni, Galileo was able to cut down the price of producing the compasses, and he also started charging buyers for instructions on how to use them. In 1606, he published *Le Operazioni del Compasso Geometrico et Militare*, an operating manual for the compass.

While teaching in Padua, Galileo made many trips to various parts of Europe, and though he usually spent his time in different towns comparing notes with other scientists, he did not confine himself strictly to business. Sometime in the years of the 16th century, while visiting Venice, he met Marina di Andrea Gamba. The two soon fell in love and Marina followed him back to Padua. For reasons known only to him, Galileo opted never to marry her but instead kept her in his home as his mistress for the rest of her life. This was particularly scandalous in heavily Catholic Padua, and those who rejected his work or disliked him personally frequently made mention of the relationship. According to one famous legend attributed to the contemporary writer Fabbroni, when some men pointed out the existence of Galileo's relationship to the Senate of Padua, they responded by increasing his salary because "he had a family to support, [and] he had the more need of an increased salary." Regardless of whether that story was true, the politicians in Padua were fully aware that Galileo's reputation and position in the city benefited Padua itself. Galileo was so popular that he occasionally had to teach outside because his classroom only had space for 1,000 students at a time.

The first of Galileo's children, Virginia, was born on August 16, 1600. She would later be considered one of the most intelligent women of her time, and she would remain her father's staunchest supporter throughout his life. Virginia and her younger sister Livia, born the following year, later became nuns and lived in a convent, where the stigmatizing taint of illegitimacy could not harm her. Their brother, Vincenzo, born in 1606, would later be legitimized by their father and made his heir.

A painting believed to depict Galileo's daughter Virginia

Chapter 3: Revolutionary Astronomy

"My dear Kepler, what would you say of the learned here, who, replete with the pertinacity of the asp, have steadfastly refused to cast a glance through the telescope? What shall we make of this? Shall we laugh, or shall we cry?" – Galileo, 1610

By 1610, Galileo had made such a name for himself in Padua that he eventually attracted the attention of the famous Medici family. He was summoned to the Italian court to share his findings with those in attendance there. In an unusual move for a man of his position, Galileo took his two daughters with him and left behind Marina and 4 year old Vincenzo. When Marina died two years later, Vincenzo joined Galileo at court.

Galileo had new patrons, but he was still unusually blunt and not afraid to ask for more of the Medici family. He reportedly told them, "I say nothing on the amount of my salary; being convinced that, as I am to live upon it, the graciousness of his highness would not deprive me of any of those comforts, of which, however, I feel the want of less than many others; and, therefore, I say nothing more on the subject. Finally, on the title and profession of my service, I should wish that, to the title of mathematician, his highness would add that of philosopher, as I profess to have studied a greater number of years in philosophy, than months in pure mathematics; and how I have profited by it, and if I can or ought to deserve this title, I may let their highnesses see, as often as it shall please them to give me an opportunity of discussing such subjects in their presence with those who are most esteemed in this knowledge."

Galileo had previously shown his interest in astronomy, but it was during his time as a patron of Cosimo II de' Medici (who he also tutored) that he truly began to focus his efforts on the heavens. In 1609, Galileo built his first telescope after figuring out the interaction between convex and concave lenses and basing his design on the work done by Hans Lippershey over the previous years. Galileo's first telescope had a limited 3X magnification that made it more like a modern spyglass than a telescope. However, it showed what could be done and inspired him to keep working. In August of that same year, he showed off a telescope with an 8X magnification to a group of government officials in Venice. They were interested and bought several, opening the door for a new lucrative business for Galileo during the years that followed. The new surge in interest also compelled Padua to name Galileo a professor for life and nearly double his salary to 1,000 florins. Meanwhile, Galileo eventually perfected a telescope design with a 30X magnification.

Cosimo II de' Medici

Giuseppe Bertini's fresco depicting Galileo using a telescope before the Duke of Venice.

A replica of Galileo's telescope

The following year he published the brief treatise *Siderus Nuncius* (*The Starry Messenger*), a description of what he had been able to observe with his new invention. First, he described what his telescope revealed about the Milky Way. To the naked eye, this part of the sky appears to be nothing more than a dust shadow across the heavens. However, using even his most primitive telescope, Galileo was able to see dozens of tiny and separate points of light that twinkled. He also noted that these stars were different sized points of light that did not move, suggesting (correctly) they were stars and not planets. Galileo could make out the disc shapes of the planets, but the stars didn't have a discernible shape, which further led him to his conclusion that they were not planets. However, Galileo's very confident style of writing turned off many readers because it came across as belittling with passages like, "What was observed by us in the third place is the nature or matter of the Milky Way itself, which, with the aid of the spyglass, may be observed so well that all the disputes that for so many generations have vexed philosophers are destroyed by visible certainty, and we are liberated from wordy arguments." Naturally, when Galileo insisted he had so thoroughly refuted past theories that his own theory was above being argued itself, it didn't sit well with others.

Part of the Milky Way from Earth

Galileo made waves with his observation of the Moon, which was visible to the naked eye on most nights of the year and looked mostly smooth and white, albeit with a few visible pockmarks. Using his telescope, as well as his understanding of light and shadows, Galileo was able to determine the existence of mountain ranges, hollows, and other physical features that indicated the Moon was anything but smooth on the surface. He could determine this by seeing the sunlight shining off high points on the Moon's surface, while nearby areas were still shrouded in darkness. Of course, when Galileo wrote a detailed description of the Moon, it flew in the face of Aristotle's teachings and laws of Nature, leaving many of Aristotle's followers to discount Galileo's work.

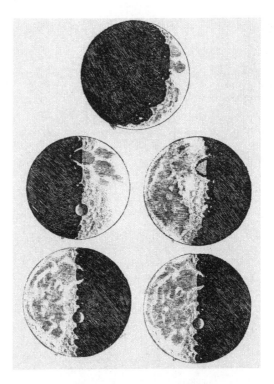

Galileo's sketches of the Moon

At the time, the most controversial of Galileo's findings concerned the four moons that Galileo saw orbiting Jupiter. Having initially observed three of them on January 7, 1610, Galileo simply thought that they were stars to the east and west of Jupiter, but he noticed the next day that their alignment had changed; they were now all to the west of Jupiter and closer to each other. When they were to the east of Jupiter a few days earlier, Galileo had verified that the bodies he initially thought were stars were in motion, eliminating the possibility that the movements could have been explained by Jupiter's motion. He wisely named them the "Medicean Stars" after his patron, but they are now called the Galilean moons. From the standpoint of Ptolemy's geocentric system, the Earth, as the center of the universe, is orbited by the sun, planets, stars and, the moon. However, Galileo had observed moons orbiting another planet, and Jupiter ostensibly had more moons orbiting it than the Earth at that. This called into question the geocentric model, at least among scientists who were willing to question authority. Kepler was so excited by Galileo's findings that he exclaimed:

"Such a fit of wonder seized me at a report which seemed to be so very absurd, and I was thrown into such agitation at seeing an old dispute between us decided in this way, that between his joy, my colouring, and the laughter of both, confounded as we were by such a novelty, we were hardly capable, he of speaking, or I of listening. On our parting, I immediately began to think how there could be any addition to the number of the planets without overturning my 'Cosmographic Mystery,' according to which Euclid's five regular solids do not allow more than six planets round the sun.... I am so far from disbelieving the existence of the four circumjovial planets, that I long for a telescope, to anticipate you, if possible, in discovering two round Mars, as the proportion seems to require, six or eight round Saturn, and perhaps one each round Mercury and Venus."

The moons Galileo saw (from top to bottom): Io, Europa, Ganymede, and Callisto. Today they're called the Galilean moons.

Galileo's notes on Jupiter's moons.

Proponents of the old system were defiant. One of Kepler's own protégés, a man named Horky, wrote against Galileo and asserted that he "would never concede his four new planets to that Italian from Padua, even if [he] should die for it." Horky had trained a telescope on Jupiter and argued that Galileo hadn't spotted anything new except for reflections of light. Kepler himself admonished Horky and used a telescope to show him that Galileo was correct, going so far as to tell Horky that he would only continue working with Horky once the man admitted Galileo was right.

On the other hand, Galileo had to deal with copycats who tried to claim his discoveries as their own. An astronomer named Thomas Harriot claimed to have found Jupiter's four moons a month earlier, and on top of that several people came forward and claimed that they had seen even more satellites around Jupiter. Later studies of Harriot's writings indicated he saw Jupiter's satellites in October 1710, well after Galileo.

Harriot

Meanwhile, Galileo was also studying other planets. Later that year, Galileo made further studies of the phases of Venus that he believed confirmed Copernicus' heliocentric solar system model. If the Earth was at the center of the universe, then Venus should disappear from Galileo's sight at certain times of the year while it orbited. But if the Earth and Venus were moving around the Sun, Venus would appear in different phases depending on its position relative to the Sun. Galileo's observation of the different phases of Venus, which he likened to the phases of the Moon, indeed suggested a heliocentric solar system.

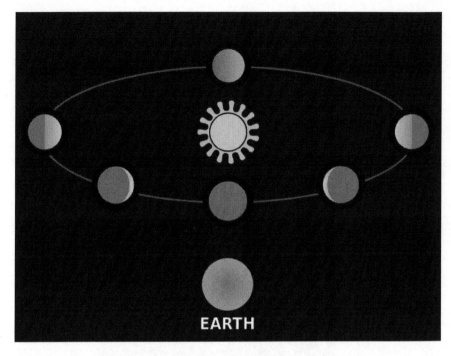

The different phases of Venus as Galileo observed

Galileo was also the first to observe Saturn's rings, which he initially mistook to be 2 other planets. Near the end of 1610, he sent the German Emperor the following riddle: "I have observed that the most remote planet is triple." However, Galileo would have to recalibrate that discovery when he noticed that Saturn's "appendages" seemed to disappear when he observed the planet at different times.

In 1611, Galileo was feted at a banquet thrown in his honor by Prince Federico Cesti. The purpose of the event was to induct Galileo into the Accademia dei Lincei (Lincean Academy), the Italian science academy formed by Cesi a few years earlier. While they were eating, a Greek mathematician, Giovanni Demisiani, rose to his feet and toasted the new "telescope," forming the word from the Greek words tele (far) and skopein (to see). But Galileo didn't use his new telescope just to see far away. He also used it to see things that were very small. For instance, his scientific journals from this period feature detailed drawing of insect limbs as he saw them through his telescope. Years later, he would modify the telescope to create the first microscope.

In 1612, Galileo came up with yet another application for his astronomical discoveries. After observing Jupiter's moons orbiting the planet at a consistent pace, he posited that their positions would allow for a new type of universal clock. He further proposed that they could be measured from various points on Earth to determine longitude. These ideas would later be refined and used by others, but Galileo would never perfect their use in his lifetime.

Furthermore, Galileo took another swing at Aristotle's teachings. In 1612, he wrote *Discourse on Bodies of Water*, which rejected Aristotle's theory that objects floated because of their shape. Instead, Galileo correctly theorizes that an object of any shape would float as long as the weight of the object was less than that of the water it displaced. He also refuted Aristotle's claim that the Sun was a perfect sphere by training his telescope on it, a practice that's now known to be quite dangerous. It was not a smooth ball of light like people thought, as demonstrated by Galileo's view of sunspots. Sunspots show up when part of the Sun's surface is not as hot as nearby parts of the Sun's surface.

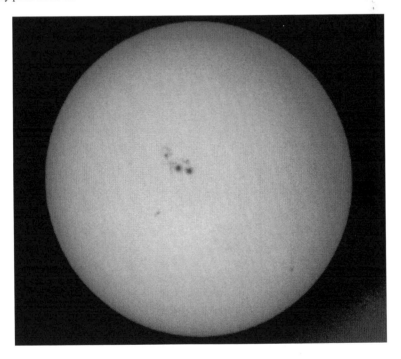

A 2004 picture of sunspots.

Galileo Before the Holy Office, **a painting by Joseph-Nicolas Robert-Fleury.**

"I do not feel obliged to believe that the same God who has endowed us with senses, reason, and intellect has intended us to forgo their use and by some other means to give us knowledge which we can attain by them…I would say here something that was heard from an ecclesiastic of the most eminent degree: 'The intention of the Holy Spirit is to teach us how one goes to heaven, not how the heavens go.'" – Galileo, Letter to the Grand Duchess Christina, 1615.

As Galileo's astronomical discoveries made their way around Europe, plenty of people began to wonder how Galileo's works could be squared with the traditional teachings of the Catholic Church. For Galileo, there was no conflict between his faith and his findings. In 1613, he wrote a letter to one of his students in which he posited his belief that the Copernican theory did not contradict Holy Scriptures or mean it was wrong; instead, he believed science offered a perspective on the heavens that was more accurate than the one described in the Bible. However, even that sounded presumptuous, and the letter found its way to the hands of the church hierarchy and eventually the Inquisition, who later brought charges of heresy against him.

Benedetto Castelli, a monk and friend of Galileo's, wrote to him in late 1613, concerned about what he was hearing. Galileo's reply clarified his stand on Copernicus' theory and the Bible.

"...it seems to me very prudent of her to propose and of you to concede and to agree that the Holy Scripture can never lie or err, and that its declarations are absolutely and inviolably true. I should have added only that, through the Scripture cannot err, nevertheless some of its interpreters and expositors can sometimes err in various ways. One of these would be very serious and very frequent, namely to want to limit oneself always to the literal meaning of the words; for there would thus emerge not only various contradictions but also serious heresies and blasphemies, and it would be necessary to attribute to God feet, hands and eyes, as well as bodily and human feelings like anger, regret, hate and sometimes even forgetfulness of things past and ignorance of future ones. Thus in the Scripture one finds many propositions which look different from the truth if one goes by the literal meaning of the words, but which are expressed in this manner to accommodate the incapacity of common people; likewise, for the few who deserve to be separated from the masses, it is necessary that wise interpreters produce their true meaning and indicate the particular reasons why they have been expressed by means of such words.

Thus, given that in many places the Scripture is not only capable but necessarily in need of interpretations different from the apparent meaning of the words, it seems to me that in disputes about natural phenomena it should be reserved to the last place. For the Holy Scripture and nature both equally derive from the divine Word, the former as the dictation of the Holy Spirit, the latter as the most obedient executrix of God's commands; moreover, in order to adapt itself to the understanding of all people, it was appropriate for the Scripture to say many things which are different from absolute truth, in appearance and in regard to the meaning of the words; on the other hand, nature is inexorable and immutable, and she does not care at all whether or not her recondite reasons and modes of operations are revealed to human understanding, and so she never transgresses the terms of the laws imposed on her; therefore, whatever sensory experience places before our eyes or necessary demonstrations prove to us concerning natural effects should not in any way be called into question on account of scriptural passages whose words appear to have a different meaning, since not every statement of the Scripture is bound to obligations as severely as each effect of nature."

Galileo then confirmed his commitment to both his faith and his reason in his letter to Castelli:

"I should believe that the authority of the Holy Writ has merely the aim of persuading men of those article and propositions which are necessary for their salvation and surpass all human reason, and so could not become credible through some other science or any other means except the mouth of the Holy Spirit itself. However, I do not think it necessary to believe that the same God who has furnished us with senses, language, and intellect would want to bypass their use and give us by other means the information we can obtain with them. This applies especially to those sciences about which one can read only very small phrases and scattered conclusions in the Scripture, as is particularly the case for astronomy, of which it contains such a small portion that one does not even find in it the names of all the planets; but if the first sacred writers had been thinking of persuading the people about the arrangement and the movements of the heavenly bodies, they would not have treated of them so sparsely, which is to say almost nothing in comparison to the infinity of very lofty and admirable conclusions contained in such a science."

Finally, Galileo took the argument a step further and addressed the concerns raised about the impact of his finding on a particular passage of Scripture. In Joshua 10, the story is told of the day God, at Joshua's request, caused the sun to stand still for a day. Traditional teaching interpreted this passage literally, as the sun not moving in its normal path around the Earth. However, Galileo had a different take on the issue, writing:

"To confirm this I now come to examining the specific passage of Joshua, concerning which you put forth three theses for their Most Serene Highness. I take the third one, which you advanced as mine (as indeed it is), but I add some other consideration that I do not believe I have ever told you.

Let us then assume and concede to the opponent that the words of the sacred text should be taken precisely in their literal meaning, namely that in answer to Joshua's prayers God made the sun stop and lengthened the day, so that as a result he achieved victory; but I request that the same rule should apply to both, so that the opponent should not pretend to tie me and to leave himself free to change or modify the meanings of the words. Given this, I say that this passage shows clearly the falsity and impossibility of the Aristotelian and Ptolemaic world system, and on the other hand agrees very well with the Copernican one.

I first ask the opponent whether he knows with how many motions the sun moves. If he knows, he must answer that is moves with two motions, namely with the annual motion from west to east and with the diurnal motion in the opposite direction from east to west.

Then, secondly, I ask him whether these two motions, so different and almost contrary to each other, belong to the sun and are its own to an equal extent. The answer must be No, but that only one is specifically its own, namely the annual motion, whereas the other is not but belongs to the highest heaven, I mean the Prime Mobile; the latter carries along with it the sun as well as the other planets and the stellar sphere, forcing them to make a revolution around the earth in twenty-four hours, with a motion, as I said, almost contrary to their own natural motion.

Coming to the third question, I ask him with which of these two motions the sun produces night and day, that is, whether with its own motion or else with that of the Prime Mobile. The answer must be that night and day are effects of the motion of the Prime Mobile and that what depends on the sun's own motion is not night or day but the various seasons and the year itself.

Now, if the day derives not from the sun's motion but from that of the Prime Mobile, who does not see that to lengthen the day one must stop the Prime Mobile and not the sun? Indeed, is there anyone who understands these first elements of astronomy and does not know that, if God had stopped the sun's motion, He would have cut and shortened the day instead of lengthening it? For, the sun's motion being contrary to the diurnal turning, the more the sun moves toward the east the more its progression toward the west is slowed down, whereas by its motion being diminished or annihilated the sun would set that much sooner; this phenomenon is observed in the moon, whose diurnal revolutions are slower than those of the sun inasmuch as its own motion is faster than that of the sun. It follows that it is absolutely impossible to stop the sun and lengthen the day in the system of Ptolemy and Aristotle, and therefore either the motions must not be arranged as Ptolemy says or we must modify the meaning of the words of the Scripture; we would have to claim that, when it says that God stopped the sun, it meant to say that He stopped the Prime Mobile, and that is said the contrary of what it would have said if speaking to educated men in order to adapt itself to the capacity of those who are barely able to understand the rising and setting of the sun.

Add to this that it is not believable that God would stop only the sun, letting the other spheres proceed; for He would have unnecessarily altered and upset all the order, appearances, and arrangements of the other stars in relation to the sun, and would have greatly disturbed the whole system of nature. On the other hand, it is believable that He would stop the whole system of celestial spheres, which could then together return to their operations without any confusion or change after the period of intervening rest.

However, we have already agreed not to change the meaning of the words in the text; therefore it is necessary to resort to another arrangement of the parts of the world, and to see whether the literal meaning of the words flows directly and without obstacle from its point of view. This is in fact what we see happening.

For I have discovered and conclusively demonstrated that the solar globe turns on itself, completing an entire rotation in about one lunar month, in exactly the same direction as all the other heavenly revolutions; moreover, it is very probable and reasonable that, as the chief instrument and minister of nature and almost the heart of the world, the sun gives not only light (as it obviously does) but also motion to all the planets that revolve around it; hence, if in conformity with Copernicus's position the diurnal motion is attributed to the earth, anyone can see that is sufficed stopping the sun to stop the whole system, and thus to lengthen the period of the diurnal illumination without altering in any way the rest of the mutual relationships of the planets; and that is exactly how the words of the sacred text sound. Here then is the manner in which by stopping the sun one can lengthen the day on the earth, without introducing any confusion among the parts of the world and without altering the words of the Scripture."

In 1615, Galileo wrote a letter to one of his benefactors, the Grand Duchess Christina. In this letter, which is really more like a short book on the subject, he again defended his scientific findings in light of Scripture. But this time, his writing was far more caustic, an indication that it greatly irritated him to have people he deemed ignorant attacking him:

"Some years ago, as Your Serene Highness well knows, I discovered in the heavens many things that had not been seen before our own age. The novelty of these things, as well as some consequences which followed from them in contradiction to the physical notions commonly held among academic philosophers, stirred up against me no small number of professors — as if I had placed these things in the sky with my own hands in order to upset nature and overturn the sciences. They seemed to forget that the increase of known truths stimulates the investigation, establishment, and growth of the arts; not their diminution or destruction...

The passage of time has revealed to everyone the truths that I previously set forth; and, together with the truth of the facts, there has come to light the great difference in attitude between those who simply and dispassionately refused to admit the discoveries to be true, and those who combined with their incredulity some reckless passion of their own. Men who were well grounded in astronomical and physical science were persuaded as soon as they received my first message. There were others who denied them or remained in doubt only because of their novel and unexpected character, and because they had not yet had the opportunity to see for themselves. These men have by degrees come to be satisfied. But some, besides allegiance to their original error, possess I know not what fanciful interest in remaining hostile not so much toward the things in question as toward their discoverer. No longer being able to deny them, these men now take refuge in obstinate silence, but being more than ever exasperated by that which has pacified and quieted other men, they divert their thoughts to other fancies and seek new ways to damage me. ... To this end they make a shield of their hypocritical zeal for religion. They go about invoking the Bible, which they would have minister to their deceitful purposes. Contrary to the sense of the Bible and the intention of the holy Fathers, if I am not mistaken, they would extend such authorities until even in purely physical matters — where faith is not involved — they would have us altogether abandon reason and the evidence of our senses in favor of some biblical passage, though under the surface meaning of its words this passage may contain a different sense...

Persisting in their original resolve to destroy me and everything mine by any means they can think of, these men are aware of my views in astronomy and philosophy. They know that as to the arrangement of the parts of the universe, I hold the sun to be situated motionless in the center of the revolution of the celestial orbs while the earth revolves about the sun. They know also that I support this position not only by refuting the arguments of Ptolemy and Aristotle, but by producing many counter-arguments; in particular, some which relate to physical effects whose causes can perhaps be assigned in no other way. In addition there are astronomical arguments derived from many things in my new celestial discoveries that plainly confute the Ptolemaic system while admirably agreeing with and confirming the contrary hypothesis.

After an exhaustive discussion, he concluded by again confirming his faith in the teachings of the Catholic Church.

"As to other scriptural passages which seem to be contrary to this opinion, I have no doubt that if the opinion itself were known to be true and proven, those very theologians who, so long as they deem it false, hold these passages to be incapable of harmonious exposition with it, would find interpretations for them which would agree very well, and especially if they would add some knowledge to astronomical science to their knowledge of divinity. At present, while they consider it false, they think they find in Scripture only passages that contradict it; but if they once entertained a different view of the matter they would probably find as many more that would harmonize with it. And then they might judge that it is fitting for the holy Church to tell that God placed the sun in the center of heaven, and that by rotating it like a wheel gave to the moon and the other wandering stars their appointed courses, when she sings the hymn:

> 'Most Holy God of Heaven
> Who paints with fiery splendor
> The brilliant center of the pole
> Enriched with beauteous light;
> Who, creating on the fourth day
> The flaming disk of the sun
> Gave order to the moon
> And wandering courses to the stars....'

And they could say that the name 'firmament' agrees literally quite well with the starry sphere and all that lies beyond the revolutions of the planets, which according to this arrangement is quite firm and immovable. Again, with the earth turning, they might think of its poles when they read *He had not yet made the earth, the rivers, and the hinges of the terrestrial orb*, for hinges would seem to be ascribed in vain to the earth unless it needed them to turn upon."

Grand Duchess Christina

Unfortunately, not everyone was satisfied with Galileo's explanations. In 1616, the Inquisition ruled that any theory purporting a heliocentric universe was inconsistent with both philosophy and theology, and thus heretical. Pope Paul V sent Cardinal Bellarmine to warn Galileo not to pursue that line of thought any further. Furthermore, the Church placed *De revolutionibus orbium coelestium*, Copernicus' book on the heliocentric model, on their List of Prohibited Books.

In an effort to be obedient to the church, Galileo complied, but no one prohibited Galileo from talking about the idea, as long as he was careful to keep all discussions theoretical. He also kept engaging in controversial conversations, one of which in Rome was described by a contemporary: "Your eminence would be delighted with Galileo if you heard him holding forth, as he often does, in the midst of fifteen or twenty, all violently attacking him, sometimes in one house, sometimes in another. But he is armed after such fashion that he laughs all of them to scorn; and even if the novelty of his opinions prevents entire persuasion, he at least convicts of emptiness most of the arguments with which his adversaries endeavour to overwhelm him. He was particularly admirable on Monday last in the house of Signor Frederico Ghisilieri; and what especially pleased me was, that before replying to the contrary arguments, he amplified and enforced them with new grounds of great plausibility, so as to leave his adversaries in a more ridiculous plight, when he afterwards overturned them all." Obviously, nothing could keep Galileo from thinking about what he had learned. That is how he occupied his mind and time over the next 7 years.

By now, Galileo was growing both older and tired of all the controversy. In 1617, he moved close to his daughters' convent near Bellosguardo, a small town west of Florence. This let him visit them more often. In 1619, Galileo filed a request to have his son Vincenzo recognized as his legal and rightful heir. Like his father and grandfather before him, Vincenzo was an excellent musician and enjoyed a successful career as a lutenist.

However, Galileo's attempts to stay out of the Church's crosshairs could only last so long. Galileo found himself in yet another controversy with a high ranking church official, Father Orazio Grassi, who was also a member of the mathematics department at the Collegio Romano. Father Grassi, a Jesuit, had written a short essay entitled *An Astronomical Disputation on the Three Comets of the Year 1618*. In it, he put forth his theory that comets moved through the universe in a circular motion, always maintaining the same distance from the Earth. Though he published the tract anonymously, everyone in the scientific community knew he had written it.

It was one thing for Galileo to let the Church prevent him from publishing controversial theories, but he couldn't stay silent while Church officials published theories that he believed were wrong. Galileo took issue with Grassi's findings and replied with his own treatise, *Discourse on the Comets*, in 1619. Although it was published by Mario Guiducci, a lawyer and disciple of Galileo's, everyone believed that Galileo had written it himself. Moreover, Galileo's treatise was polemic in nature, and it concentrated more on attacking Grassi than offering up his own explanation. He also attacked others in the treatise, particularly a Jesuit named Christopher Scheiner.

After he insulted one of the most influential orders in the Church, Galileo was in hot water again. In 1621, a "pupil" by the name of Lothario Sarsi responded to Galileo's claims with *The Astronomical and Philosophical Balance*. Galileo, seeing that this latest salvo was obviously written by Grassi, responded with *Il Saggiatore* (*The Assayer*), in 1623. Considered by many to be his "scientific manifesto," it is a treatise not just about his own research but also about his scientific method. In other words, long before Descartes wrote *The Scientific Method*, Galileo put forth an argument about how all scientists should work, encouraging them to conduct research and experimentation instead of guess work and superstition. He wrote, "Philosophy is written in that great book which ever lies before our eyes — I mean the universe — but we cannot understand it if we do not first learn the language and grasp the symbols, in which it is written. This book is written in the mathematical language, and the symbols are triangles, circles and other geometrical figures, without whose help it is impossible to comprehend a single word of it; without which one wanders in vain through a dark labyrinth."

At the same time, he recognized the limitations of the even the scientific method, concluding:

"As soon as I think of a material object or a corporeal substance, I immediately feel the need to conceive that it is bounded and has this or that shape, that it is big or small in relation to others, that it is in this or that place at a given time, that it moves or stays still, that it touches or does not touch another body, and that it is one, few, or many. I cannot separate it from these conditions by any stretch of my imagination. But my mind feels no compulsion to understand as necessary accompaniments that it should be white or red, bitter or sweet, noisy or silent, of sweet or of foul odor. Indeed, without the senses to guide us, reason or imagination alone would perhaps never arrive at such qualities. I think that tastes, odors, colors and the like are no more than mere names so far as pertains to the subject wherein they seem to reside, and that they only exist in the body that perceives them. Thus, if all living creatures were removed, all these qualities would also be removed and annihilated."

While the book is memorable for advocating a scientific method based on empiricism, it was also Galileo's finest work as a polemic. He scathingly added, "Long experience has taught me this about the status of mankind with regard to matters requiring thought: the less people know and understand about them, the more positively they attempt to argue concerning them, while on the other hand to know and understand a multitude of things renders men cautious in passing judgment upon anything new."

Book cover for *The Assayer*

Though the Jesuits were not happy about this latest insult, there was little that they could do. By this time, Galileo's friend, Cardinal Maffeo Barberini, had been elected Pope Urban VIII. Barberini had opposed the Inquisition's earlier decision and remained open to whatever Galileo wished to discuss. In fact, Galileo had dedicated the work to the newest Pope, and Urban VIII was pleased with it.

Pope Urban VIII

Galileo also worked during this time on a number of experiments and inventions that offended no one. For instance, he continued to refine his attempts to convert a telescope into a microscope, and when he improved it in 1624, he gave some of them to the Duke of Bavaria and other friends, including Prince Cesi. The new tool had no name, but as they had with the telescope, the Linceans rose to task. Giovanni Faber said that it should be called a microscope, from the Greek micron (small) and skopein (to look at). The following year, an entomologist used the microscope to make some of the earliest drawings of insect limbs ever published.

Encouraged, Galileo published *Dialogue Concerning the Two Chief World Systems* in 1632. He had been told he could publish about different theories of the solar system by Pope Urban, under two conditions. The first was that he had to present arguments both for and against the heliocentric model. Then Urban asked that his own thoughts, representing those of the Church, be included too.

Galileo complied, but in a way that sparked controversy. The work reads like a conversation between three men: Salvian, Sagredo, and Simplicius. Although he tried to present both evidence in favor and against the heliocentric model, he named the character who was presenting the evidence against Copernicus' theory Simplicius. Though Simplicius was ostensibly based off of a respected ancient philosopher of the same name, it also seemed that Galileo was not so subtly calling those who opposed his ideas simpletons by extension. Worse than that, he wrote the book in such a way that Simplicius' ideas were often defeated or seemed foolish. For example, Sagredo speaks about the notion of the universe being inalterable in a way that lambasted Simplicius:

> "I cannot without great astonishment — I might say without great insult to my intelligence — hear it attributed as a prime perfection and nobility of the natural and integral bodies of the universe that they are invariant, immutable, inalterable, etc., while on the other hand it is called a great imperfection to be alterable, generable, mutable, etc. For my part I consider the earth very noble and admirable precisely because of the diverse alterations, changes, generations, etc. that occur in it incessantly. If, not being subject to any changes, it were a vast desert of sand or a mountain of jasper, or if at the time of the flood the waters which covered it had frozen, and it had remained an enormous globe of ice where nothing was ever born or ever altered or changed, I should deem it a useless lump in the universe, devoid of activity and, in a word, superfluous and essentially non-existent. This is exactly the difference between a living animal and a dead one; and I say the same of the moon, of Jupiter, and of all other world globes."

Meanwhile, Salviati seems to take aim at the notion that scientists could allow themselves to believe something that their own scientific method rejects:

> "If what we are discussing were a point of law or of the humanities, in which neither true nor false exists, one might trust in subtlety of mind and readiness of tongue and in the greater experience of the writers, and expect him who excelled in those things to make his reasoning most plausible, and one might judge it to be the best. But in the natural sciences, whose conclusions are true and necessary and have nothing to do with human will, one must take care not to place oneself in the defense of error; for here a thousand Demostheneses and a thousand Aristotles would be left in the lurch by every mediocre wit who happened to hit upon the truth for himself. Therefore, Simplicius, give up this idea and this hope of yours that there may be men so much more learned, erudite, and well-read than the rest of us as to be able to make that which is false become true in defiance of nature."

Finally, Galileo's treatise seems to fire a shot right across the bow of the Church, which had suppressed Copernicus' writings and were trying to suppress his own:

> "In the long run my observations have convinced me that some men, reasoning preposterously, first establish some conclusion in their minds which, either because of its being their own or because of their having received it from some person who has their entire confidence, impresses them so deeply that one finds it impossible ever to

get it out of their heads. Such arguments in support of their fixed idea as they hit upon themselves or hear set forth by others, no matter how simple and stupid these may be, gain their instant acceptance and applause. On the other hand whatever is brought forward against it, however ingenious and conclusive, they receive with disdain or with hot rage — if indeed it does not make them ill. Beside themselves with passion, some of them would not be backward even about scheming to suppress and silence their adversaries."

Not surprisingly, Pope Urban was not amused by what he considered a betrayal. By this time, word had reached the pontiff's ears that there were men around him conspiring against his authority. Furthermore, some of the Spanish Cardinals, backers of the infamous Spanish Inquisition, went as far as to accuse him of being too soft on heresy, which by extension was an accusation that he was being lenient on heretics themselves.

In September 1632, Galileo received a letter summoning him to Rome to stand trial before the Inquisition. As an institution, the Catholic Inquisition dated to the 12th century, and various forms of the Inquisition would be maintained by Protestants and Catholics alike for centuries. Today it is most commonly associated with the horrors of the Spanish Inquisition during the late 15th century, but the Roman Inquisition was hardly benevolent itself.

At first, Galileo hoped that Urban might intervene on his behalf, but the Pontiff no longer had the clout or the inclination to protect him. Thus, he finally made the trip in early 1633, arriving in the Eternal City in February of that year. Once he reached Rome, he was charged by Vincenzo Maculani, the inquisitor, of heresy for continuing to teach that the sun was the center of the universe. Though he maintained during the early days of his trial that he had not done anything of the kind since 1616, he did finally admit that someone reading the *Dialogue* would most likely be persuaded that Copernicus' theory was the correct one. By this time, he was no longer being treated with the respect he had originally received, and he was fully aware he could be tortured or even executed.

Cristiano Banti's 1857 painting of Galileo talking to the Inquisition

Galileo was before the Inquisition for 18 days, and on June 22, 1633, the court delivered its verdict. First, Galileo was forced to recant his earlier statements, which he did in the following statement, signed by him that day:

"I, Galileo, son of the late Vincenzo Galilei, Florentine, aged seventy years, arraigned personally before this tribunal, and kneeling before you, Most Eminent and Reverend Lord Cardinals, Inquisitors-General against heretical depravity throughout the entire Christian commonwealth, having before my eyes and touching with my hands, the Holy Gospels, swear that I have always believed, do believe, and by God's help will in the future believe, all that is held, preached, and taught by the Holy Catholic and Apostolic Church. But whereas -- after an injunction had been judicially intimated to me by this Holy Office, to the effect that I must altogether abandon the false opinion that the sun is the center of the world and immovable, and that the earth is not the center of the world, and moves, and that I must not hold, defend, or teach in any way whatsoever, verbally or in writing, the said false doctrine, and after it had been notified to me that the said doctrine was contrary to Holy Scripture -- I wrote and printed a book in which I discuss this new doctrine already condemned, and adduce arguments of great cogency in its favor, without presenting any solution of these, and for this reason I have been pronounced by the Holy Office to be vehemently suspected of heresy, that is to say, of having held and believed that the Sun is the center of the world and immovable, and that the earth is not the center and moves:

Therefore, desiring to remove from the minds of your Eminences, and of all faithful Christians, this vehement suspicion, justly conceived against me, with sincere heart and unfeigned faith I abjure, curse, and detest the aforesaid errors and heresies, and generally every other error, heresy, and sect whatsoever contrary to the said Holy Church, and I swear that in the future I will never again say or assert, verbally or in writing, anything that might furnish occasion for a similar suspicion regarding me; but that should I know any heretic, or person suspected of heresy, I will denounce him to this Holy Office, or to the Inquisitor or Ordinary of the place where I may be. Further, I swear and promise to fulfill and observe in their integrity all penances that have been, or that shall be, imposed upon me by this Holy Office. And, in the event of my contravening, (which God forbid) any of these my promises and oaths, I submit myself to all the pains and penalties imposed and promulgated in the sacred canons and other constitutions, general and particular, against such delinquents. So help me God, and these His Holy Gospels, which I touch with my hands.

I, the said Galileo Galilei, have abjured, sworn, promised, and bound myself as above; and in witness of the truth thereof I have with my own hand subscribed the present document of my abjuration, and recited it word for word at Rome, in the Convent of Minerva, this twenty-second day of June, 1633.

I, Galileo Galilei, have abjured as above with my own hand."

It's understandable that Galileo would go ahead and "confess", while knowing full well that he was correct. In 1633, he was already nearly 70 years old and clearly in the twilight of life, and he had already spent much of the previous decade simply working and studying without publishing new materials. German mathematician David Hilbert may have summed Galileo's decision up best when he said, "Galileo was no idiot. Only an idiot could believe that science requires martyrdom — that may be necessary in religion, but in time a scientific result will establish itself."

Galileo's trial before the Inquisition also led to the event that he is probably best known by. According to legend, at some point after being interrogated, Galileo muttered, "And yet it moves." That reference to the Earth serves to demonstrate Galileo's defiance before the oppressive Church authorities, and his utter refusal to knowingly lie to himself or others, but the legend is almost certainly apocryphal. Its first appearance in print came a century after Galileo's death in 1754, when Italian author Giuseppe Baretti wrote, "This is the celebrated Galileo, who was in the inquisition for six years, and put to the torture, for saying, that the earth moved. The moment he was set at liberty, he looked up to the sky and down to the ground, and, stamping with his foot, in a contemplative mood, said, Eppur si move, that is, still it moves, meaning the earth." Despite the incorrect facts about the time Galileo spent before the Inquisition, this colorful legend continued to circulate widely among subsequent authors and eventually became Galileo's most famous words. For a man who wrote prolifically during his life, it was ironic that he is best remembered for something he probably never said.

That said, in the 20th century an Italian painting dating back to the 1640s had a variation of the famous legend. That painting, which incorrectly depicts Galileo being imprisoned in a dungeon, indicates that the legend of Galileo whispering "And yet it moves" under his breath dated all the way back to near the time of his death. Nevertheless, the story still had no way of being substantiated and is still almost unanimously discounted among scholars.

Despite signing the confession, Galileo was sentenced to be imprisoned for whatever period time the Inquisition saw fit, but the Inquisition sentenced him to house arrest because he confessed. All the books he had ever written were banned from further publication or use by the Catholic Church, and that included anything he might wish to publish in the future. As part of his sentence, Galileo lived with the Archbishop of Siena, Ascanio Piccolomini for some time. Piccolomini was a pleasant man, and the two got along well. In 1634, Galileo was allowed to return to his home in Arcetri, where he would live out the rest of his life under house arrest.

Now that he was old and under house arrest, one of Galileo's greatest delights was spending time with his oldest daughter, now known as the nun Maria Celeste. She had inherited her father's keen mind and assisted him with much of his work, especially after he became blind in1638. It was Maria Celeste who intervened on his behalf with the Church, getting permission to even take a small part of his sentence on her own shoulders: the reading of seven penitential psalms a week.

Meanwhile, Galileo's conflicts with the Church were not keeping him from continuing to observe experiment and write. However, when he decided to publish *Discorsi e Dimostrazioni Matematiche, intorno a due nuove scienze* (Discourses and Mathematical Demonstrations Relating to Two New Sciences) in 1638, he had to have it printed in Holland, where the Inquisition had no authority. *Two New Sciences* is considered by many to be his greatest work. In it, he presented a summary of all that he had learned during his 40 years of observation and experimentation, using the same three controversial characters that he did in the 1632 *Dialogue* (but this time Simplicius doesn't come across as a fool). It is this piece, acclaimed by such greats as Stephen Hawking and Albert Einstein, which has earned him the title Father of Modern Physics. Hawking said of it, ""So great a contribution to physics was *Two New Sciences* that scholars have long maintained that the book anticipated Isaac Newton's laws of motion." Einstein asserted, "Galileo ... is the father of modern physics — indeed of modern science."

Galileo kept working even as he got older and fell ill, but he could not help but feel aggrieved at the fact he was going blind, given how he more than anyone else had furthered people's understanding of astronomy. In July 1637, he wrote a particularly sad letter to his friend Élie Diodati, complaining, "I have been in my bed for five weeks, oppressed with weakness and other infirmities from which my age, seventy four years, permits me not to hope release. Added to this ([O misery!]) the sight of my right eye — that eye whose labors (dare I say it) have had such glorious results — is for ever lost. That of the left, which was and is imperfect, is rendered null by continual weeping." A few months later, he wrote to Diodati, "Alas! Your dear friend and servant Galileo has been for the last month hopelessly blind; so that this heaven, this earth, this universe, which I by my marvelous discoveries and clear demonstrations had enlarged a hundred thousand times beyond the belief of the wise men of bygone ages, henceforward for me is shrunk into such a small space as is filled by my own bodily sensations."

During the last years of his life, Galileo suffered from a hernia that required him to travel to Florence for medical treatment. He also found it more and more difficult to sleep at night, perhaps because he still had so much he wanted to accomplish. In 1641, he developed an irregular heartbeat. Then, around Christmas that year he contracted some sort of infection and began running a high fever. These conditions led to his death on January 8, 1642. He was 77 years old.

Though condemned by the Church, Galileo was still well respected by many powerful people. Ferdinando II, the Grand Duke of Tuscany, got permission to bury him in the Basilica of Santa Croce. The Grand Duke initially wanted him buried with great pomp in the main part of the basilica, but since Galileo's writings were still banned, he was buried in a small room near the novice's chapel. His body would later be moved to the main part of the basilica in 1737, but it would not be until 1835 that the Church lifted its ban on writings about the heliocentric model.

In January 1992, on the 350th anniversary of Galileo's death, Pope John Paul II apologized on behalf of the Catholic Church for the persecution that Galileo suffered.

Galileo's tomb in Santa Croce, Italy

Bibliography

Allan-Olney, Mary (1870). The Private Life of Galileo: Compiled primarily from his correspondence and that of his eldest daughter, Sister Maria Celeste. Boston: Nichols and Noyes.

Biagioli, Mario (1993). *Galileo, Courtier: The Practice of Science in the Culture of Absolutism.* Chicago, IL: University of Chicago Press.

Blackwell, Richard J. (2006). *Behind the Scenes at Galileo's Trial.* Notre Dame, IN: University of Notre Dame Press.

Brodrick, James, S. J. (1965). *Galileo: the man, his work, his misfortunes.* London: G. Chapman.

Clavelin, Maurice (1974). *The Natural Philosophy of Galileo.* MIT Press.

Cooper, Lane (1935). *Aristotle, Galileo, and the Tower of Pisa*. Ithaca, NY: Cornell University Press.

Drake, Stillman (1957). *Discoveries and Opinions of Galileo*. New York: Doubleday & Company.

Drake, Stillman (1970). *Galileo Studies*. Ann Arbor: The University of Michigan Press.

Drake, Stillman (1978). *Galileo At Work*. Chicago: University of Chicago Press.

Drake, Stillman (1990). *Galileo: Pioneer Scientist*. Toronto: The University of Toronto Press.

Fantoli, Annibale (2003). *Galileo: For Copernicanism and the Church* (third English ed.). Vatican Observatory Publications.

Finocchiaro, Maurice A. (1997). Galileo on the world systems: a new abridged translation and guide. Berkeley and Los Angeles, CA: University of California Press.

Finocchiaro, Maurice A. (1989). The Galileo Affair: A Documentary History. Berkeley, CA: University of California Press.

Galilei, Galileo (1960) [1623]. *The Assayer*. Translated by Stillman Drake. In Drake & O'Malley (1960, pp. 151–336).

Galilei, Galileo (1953) [1632]. *Dialogue Concerning the Two Chief World System*. Translated by Stillman Drake. Berkeley, CA: University of California Press.

Galilei, Galileo (1954) [1638, 1914]. Crew, Henry; de Salvio, Alfonso. eds. Dialogues Concerning Two New Sciences. New York, NY: Dover Publications Inc..

Galilei, Galileo *Galileo: Two New Sciences* (Translation by Stillman Drake of Galileo's 1638 *Discourses and mathematical demonstrations concerning two new sciences*) University of Wisconsin Press 1974

Galilei, Galileo, and Guiducci, Mario (1960) [1619]. *Discourse on the Comets*. Translated by Stillman Drake.

Galilei, Galileo; Scheiner, Christoph (2010). *On Sunspots*. Translated and with and introduction by Eileen Reeves and Albert Van Helden. Chicago: University of Chicago Press.

von Gebler, Karl (1879). Galileo Galilei and the Roman Curia. London: C.K. Paul & Co..

Geymonat, Ludovico (1965), *Galileo Galilei, A biography and inquiry into his philosophy and science*, translation of the 1957 Italian edition, with notes and appendix by Stillman Drake, McGraw-Hill

Gingerich, Owen (1992). *The Great Copernican Chase and other adventures in astronomical history*. Cambridge, MA: Cambridge University Press.

Grassi, Horatio (1960a) [1619]. *On the Three Comets of the Year MDCXIII*. translated by C.D. O'Malley.

Grassi, Horatio (1960b) [1619]. *The Astronomical and Philosophical Balance*. translated by C.D. O'Malley.

Hilliam, R. (2005), Galileo Galilei: Father of modern science, The Rosen Publishing Group.

Heilbron, John L. (2010). *Galileo*. New York, NY: Oxford University Press.

Koyré, Alexandre *Galilean Studies* Harvester Press 1978

Lattis, James M. (1994). *Between Copernicus and Galileo: Christopher Clavius and the Collapse of Ptolemaic Cosmology*, Chicago: the University of Chicago Press

Langford, Jerome K., O.P. (1998) [1966]. *Galileo, Science and the Church* (third ed.). St. Augustine's Press. Original edition by Desclee (New York, NY, 1966)

McMullin, Ernan, ed. (2005). *The Church and Galileo*. Notre Dame, IN: University of Notre Dame Press.

Machamer, Peter (Ed) *The Cambridge Companion to Galileo* Cambridge University Press 1998

Moss, Jean Dietz; Wallace, William (2003). Rhetoric & dialectic in the time of Galileo. Washington D.C.: CUA Press.

Reston, James (2000). *Galileo: A Life*. Beard Books.

Seeger, Raymond J. (1966). *Galileo Galilei, his life and his works*. Oxford: Pergamon Press.

Sharratt, Michael (1994). *Galileo: Decisive Innovator*. Cambridge: Cambridge University Press.

Shapere, Dudley *Galileo, a Philosophical Study* University of Chicago Press 1974

Shea, William R. and Artigas, Mario (2003). *Galileo in Rome: The Rise and Fall of a Troublesome Genius*. Oxford: Oxford University Press.

Sobel, Dava (2000) [1999]. *Galileo's Daughter*. London: Fourth Estate.

Wallace, William A. (1984) *Galileo and His Sources: The Heritage of the Collegio Romano in Galileo's Science,* (Princeton: Princeton Univ. Pr.).

Wallace, William A. (2004). *Domingo de Soto and the Early Galileo*. Aldershot: Ashgate Publishing.

White, Michael (2007). *Galileo: Antichrist: A Biography*. London: Weidenfeld & Nicolson.

Made in the USA
Middletown, DE
19 February 2022

61527388R00029